Classifying Maps

Henzel, Cynthia Kenne
ATOS BL 6.0
Points: 0.5

MW01379771

LG

On the Map

Classifying Maps

Cynthia Kennedy Henzel

ABDO
Publishing Company

visit us at
www.abdopublishing.com

Published by ABDO Publishing Company, 8000 West 78th Street, Edina, Minnesota 55439. Copyright © 2008 by Abdo Consulting Group, Inc. International copyrights reserved in all countries. No part of this book may be reproduced in any form without written permission from the publisher. The Checkerboard Library™ is a trademark and logo of ABDO Publishing Company.

Printed in the United States.

Cover Photo: AP Images
Interior Photos: Alamy p. 7; AP Images pp. 23, 28; Comstock p. 27; Corbis pp. 5, 9, 12, 14, 15; iStockphoto pp. 19, 20; Library of Congress pp. 8, 11, 13; Maps of World p. 18; National Oceanic and Atmospheric Administration/Department of Commerce pp. 26, 29; U.S. Census Bureau p. 17; Visible Earth/NASA pp. 6, 22, 24, 25

Series Coordinator: BreAnn Rumsch
Editors: Megan M. Gunderson, BreAnn Rumsch
Art Direction & Cover Design: Neil Klinepier

Library of Congress Cataloging-in-Publication Data

Henzel, Cynthia Kennedy, 1954-
 Classifying maps / Cynthia Kennedy Henzel.
    p. cm. -- (On the map)
 Includes bibliographical references and index.
 ISBN 978-1-59928-948-9
1. Maps--Juvenile literature. I. Title.

 GA105.6.H46 2008
 912--dc22
                                    2007029206

Contents

Useful Information

Maps are everywhere. You find them in your classroom, at the mall, in newspapers, on television, and in your car. Maps are everywhere because they are the best way to get information about places.

However, all of the information about a place cannot fit onto a single map. So, maps give a selective representation of a place. Selective representation means that the **cartographer** chooses only certain features to display on the map.

These choices depend on the map's purpose. The purpose may be to provide information about a place or to compare several places. Or, a map may be designed to help travelers find their way.

Maps can be helpful as long as you know what kind of map you need!

Satellite images can be effective thematic maps. City lights from around the world reveal which areas are most populated.

Reference maps show the features of a particular area. The world map in your classroom is a reference map. It gives the locations of countries, mountains, seas, and cities. A road map of Kansas and a directory of Springfield Mall are examples of reference maps for smaller areas.

Thematic maps compare information about a feature across an area. They are based on a theme or a type of information. Examples of thematic maps are "Rainforests of the World" or "Where Students Do Well." "Rainforests of the World" shows where rainforests do and do not exist. "Where Students Do Well" compares the test scores of students in different school districts.

On thematic maps, colors or patterns often show different cohorts. A cohort is a group of similar things. For example, three cohorts of students might be Fourth, Fifth, and Sixth graders.

A mall directory is a type of reference map.

Physical Maps

Physical maps are reference maps that show landforms and bodies of water. The main purpose of a physical map is to provide a general overview of an area's landscape. Physical maps may include mountains, **plains**, rivers, lakes, or oceans. They may also include vegetation, such as forests or grasslands.

Some physical maps use shading to show a **three-dimensional** view. These relief maps detail the variations and inequalities of a landscape. Darker shades may represent valleys. Bands of color may show different elevations. Some relief maps are even molded in plastic to show mountains and valleys.

Shading makes it easier to see peaks and grooves in the earth's surface.

Molded relief maps can be a realistic and fun way to study the earth's surface features.

Geologic maps are another type of physical map. These maps show the physical features of what lies beneath the earth's surface. Most physical maps allow us to identify and protect Earth's valuable resources. These maps help people use our land safely and wisely.

Topographic Maps

Topographic maps are reference maps that show the elevation and slope of the land. On a topographic map, contour lines connect points of equal elevation. So, all points on a contour line are the same distance above sea level.

On U.S. Geological Survey (USGS) maps, the contour lines appear as brown squiggles. Every five

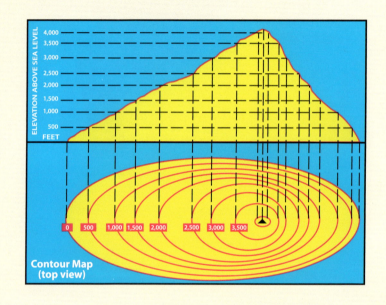

Contour Map
(top view)

lines, there is a darker line called an index contour. These bold lines are marked with the elevation they represent.

The contour interval is the distance in elevation between each contour line. This information is stated on the map near the **scale**. If the contour interval equals 20 feet (6 m), there is a

20-foot change in elevation between each contour line. So if one of the index contour lines is marked 2,000 feet (610 m), then the next line uphill indicates 2,020 (616 m) feet.

Some of the contour lines on a topographic map are close together. This means the land is rapidly changing elevation in a short distance across the ground. For example, a steep mountainside has contour lines that are close together. Fairly flat land has contour lines that are far apart. If you are hiking, very close contour lines mean you have a steep climb ahead!

A quadrangle from part of Grand Canyon National Park.

Sized to Scale

The USGS is responsible for creating most U.S. topographical maps. Their most detailed map is the quadrangle map. These maps have a scale of 1:24,000. For these maps, that means one inch (3 cm) on paper equals 24,000 inches (61,000 cm) in reality.

Quadrangle maps are also called 7.5 minute maps. This is because they cover 7.5 minutes of latitude and 7.5 minutes of longitude. This is approximately equal to an area of eight miles (13 km) north and south by six miles (10 km) east and west. However, because distance between lines of longitude varies, these maps do not always cover the same amount of land.

Political Maps

Political maps show boundaries recognized by governments. These include borders between countries, states, and school districts. Often, each political unit is shown in a different color. The names of various political units are printed on the map as well.

Political maps tell us which government or agency controls an area. Laws of different countries, states, or cities may vary. For example, students may qualify for their driver's license at different ages, depending on the state they live in. And, crossing a country line often requires a **passport**!

When you travel, a passport helps officials determine whether you live in their country or are just visiting.

This map of Europe uses colors to identify country borders. It is important to use enough colors so each country stands out.

We use political maps to show who is in charge of different services. Voters must know which **precinct** they live in to figure out where to vote. Students must know which school district they live in to attend the correct school.

Unofficial boundaries may also be mapped. Usually, these boundaries try to define the **characteristics** of a place. The Bible Belt in the southern United States is thought to have a very religious population. And in Los Angeles, California, the ZIP code 90210 is associated with wealth.

Remember to use caution when naming unofficial boundaries in your own community. They can be an unfair way to **classify** people based on where they live.

Road Maps

Road maps can help you plan a road trip or find your way to a new friend's house.

People traveling from place to place use road maps. These maps name highways and streets. Many print the distances between places on the map. That way, travelers know how far it is from one place to the next.

Some road maps show attractions that travelers might like to visit. These might include historical markers, amusement parks, or natural wonders. Road maps might also indicate where to buy gasoline and food. And, they can tell where rest stops are located.

Road maps usually have symbols for different types of roads. Larger or colored lines indicate major highways. Smaller lines show streets. Roads under construction may be shown with broken lines. A shortcut may not be the quickest route if some roads aren't built yet!

Today, people can access road maps on the Internet. Many online services provide driving directions from one location to the next. Locations of restaurants and other businesses can be shown on maps, too. Just don't forget to print your directions before leaving the house!

Population Maps

Population maps are a type of thematic map. They compare the number of people in different areas. For example, a U.S. map might show the most populated states in red and the least populated states in blue.

Population **density** maps show how crowded areas are. **Urban** areas have a high population density because many people live close together. Population density is important for government planning. Areas with high population density need more infrastructure (IHN-fruh-struhk-chuhr). This includes transportation systems, law enforcement, and schools.

State population is important information in the United States. This is because population determines the number of representatives each state has in Congress. So, an official U.S. Census is conducted every ten years to count the population.

Population maps do not just show the number of people in a given area. Many of them paint a picture of our communities. Populations may be divided into cohorts based on wealth, habits, age, or thousands of other categories. You might be in

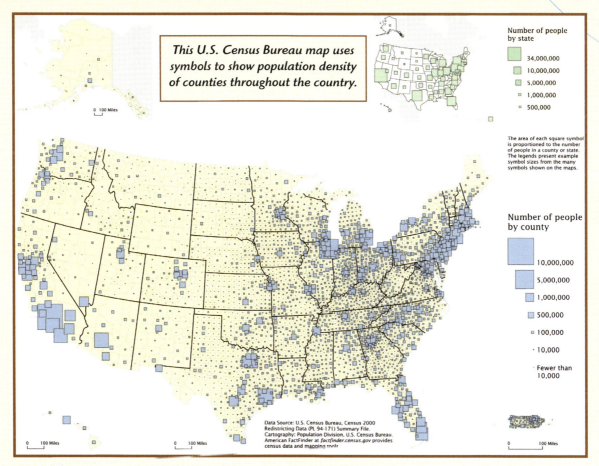

This U.S. Census Bureau map uses symbols to show population density of counties throughout the country.

Number of people by state

34,000,000
10,000,000
5,000,000
1,000,000
500,000

The area of each square symbol is proportioned to the number of people in a county or state. The legends present example symbol sizes from the many symbols shown on the maps.

Number of people by county

10,000,000
5,000,000
1,000,000
500,000
100,000
10,000
Fewer than 10,000

Data Source: U.S. Census Bureau, Census 2000 Redistricting Data (PL 94-171) Summary File. Cartography: Population Division, U.S. Census Bureau. American FactFinder at *factfinder.census.gov* provides census data and mapping tools.

a cohort of students who use computers, listen to pop music, attend church, or believe in UFOs.

Businesses use population maps to help make decisions. They need to know about the people in an area in order to determine if they can sell their products there. A toy company would not want to build a new store in a retirement community!

Economic Maps

Economic maps show the **distribution** of wealth. This includes maps that compare factors such as wages, **unemployment**, and the wealth of nations.

Some economic maps demonstrate the health of an economy. Maps of the gross domestic product (GDP) show the total goods and services produced by a nation. The GDP is used to indicate which nations are doing well and which may need financial assistance.

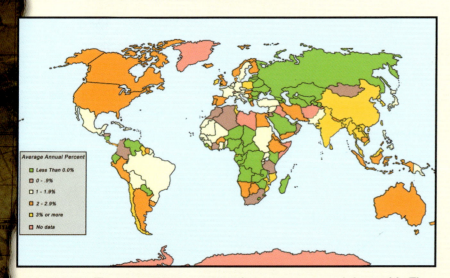

Average Annual Percent
- Less Than 0.0%
- 0 - .9%
- 1 - 1.9%
- 2 - 2.9%
- 3% or more
- No data

Maps of the consumer price index (CPI) show how much it costs to live in an area. The CPI gives an estimate of what people pay for

This map compares national economies around the world. The orange and yellow countries have the strongest growing economies.

common goods, such as groceries and fuel. It also includes the cost of Internet service, education, clothing, and eating out. If the CPI goes up, you may need an increase in your allowance!

Young people do not usually earn much money. However, they are an important part of the economy. They often have disposable income, which can be spent on luxury items such as a new video game or CD. So, businesses want to know where young people live and what they buy. By studying maps with this information, businesses can increase their sales.

Resource Maps

Resource maps are another type of thematic map. These maps show the **distribution** of things that have economic value. Petroleum, precious minerals or gems, freshwater, forests, and fisheries are useful resources to map. However, resource maps are different from economic maps.

Resource maps can provide clues about what people in an area do. For example, an area with gold or coal provides a community with jobs in the mining industry. And, regions with good soil are likely to have more farmers than other areas.

Countries with valuable resources may be wealthy. But, this is not always the case. Some places with valuable natural resources lack wealth, due to poor government. Other places choose to not use all their resources. Yet, conservation can be beneficial. For instance, national parks generate money through tourism.

An area's resources may influence whether you live near a farm or a factory.

Other resources can be mapped as well. These include assets that are not used up over time, such as education. An educated population is a valuable resource for a country. It provides skilled labor, which brings wealth to the community.

ECONOMIC RESOURCES OF PENNSYLVANIA

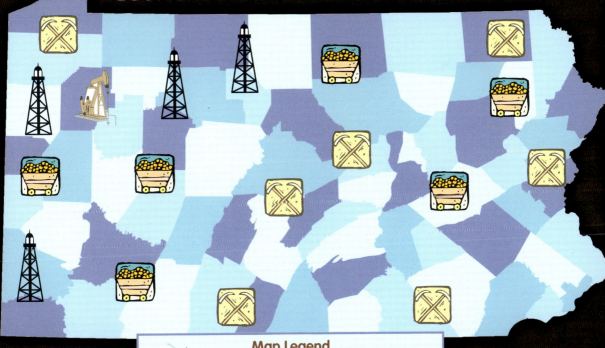

Map Legend

Natural Gas   Coal   Limestone   Oil

Environmental Maps

Some **environmental** maps show the **distribution** of plants and animals. Scientists use these maps to monitor changes in

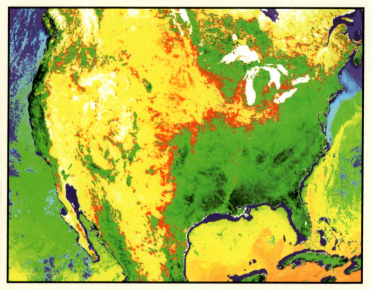

Satellite images map vegetation growth, shown in green, across the United States.

wildlife populations. In the United States, the Fish and Wildlife Service offers a mapping service that shows which **habitats** should be protected.

Other environmental maps provide information on factors that affect our health or safety. The U.S. Environmental Protection Agency is in charge of protecting human health and the environment. It tracks local air quality and issues health warnings when conditions are poor. Maps of air and water quality tell us if a place has a healthy environment.

Scientists use environmental maps to locate and track plant and animal species, as well as monitor the health of the environment.

Maps of disease outbreaks help scientists track epidemics. These **environmental** maps can warn people to take precautions in their areas and stop the spread of disease. Mapping cases of SARS, West Nile virus, and avian influenza have saved thousands of lives.

This image from space offers a different perspective of air quality than a map does. It shows how much smog rests between Earth's surface and the cloud layer over New York.

On the other hand, maps sometimes help explain why a disease is getting worse. Scientists are trying to understand why more people have been developing **asthma**. Maps could help solve this question by comparing where asthma has increased with other factors, such as chemical pollution.

Natural disaster maps show where earthquakes, floods, or hurricanes are likely to occur. You definitely want to know if you live in an area where these events take place! Governments also use these maps to help plan for disaster aid.

Scientists use climate maps to track global warming and cooling. These maps compare changes in Earth's surface temperature, climate, and vegetation over time. This shows whether deserts are growing or ice caps are melting.

Climate changes force shifts in animal and human populations. Some areas may become too dry to support crops. Others may become too warm for polar animals. So, these maps help scientists **predict** the future conditions of our climate.

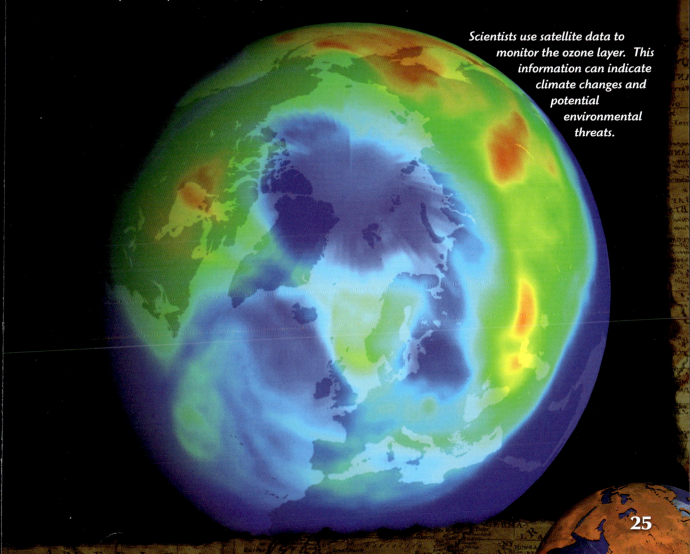

Scientists use satellite data to monitor the ozone layer. This information can indicate climate changes and potential environmental threats.

Navigational Charts

Navigational charts are maps made for finding your way at sea or in the air. Nautical charts are used for sea travel. Aeronautical charts are used by aircraft pilots.

The Office of Coast Survey (OCS) produces nautical charts for U.S. waters. The OCS uses a **hydrographic survey** to collect information about tides, currents, bottom composition, and water depth. The locations of navigational aids such as landmarks, lighted beacons, and floating buoys (BOO-eez) are

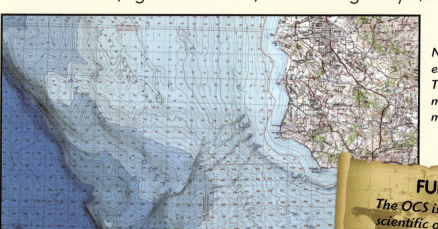

NOAA charts are extremely accurate. They show water depth, making navigation much safer.

FUN FACT

The OCS is the oldest U.S. scientific organization. It was established as the Survey of the Coast in 1807 by Thomas Jefferson. It is now part of the National Oceanic and Atmospheric Administration (NOAA).

Navigational charts ensure that pilots will not get lost on their air adventures!

marked. And underwater threats, such as shipwrecks, are carefully located.

All of this information must be continuously updated. Underwater formations and other objects along a shoreline can easily drift. So, the OCS posts weekly updates for its nautical charts. On average, the charts are completely redone every two years.

The National Aeronautical Charting Office of the Federal Aviation Administration publishes U.S. aeronautical charts. Pilots use these charts to plan their flights and navigate **accurately**.

Aeronautical charts include land, water, and man-made features that can be seen from the air. These details help pilots orient themselves with their charts while in flight. Information about airports and air traffic radio facilities is also included.

Weather Charts

Weather charts help **predict** changes in the weather. These maps show the **distribution** of **precipitation** and temperature. So, they can help you decide what to wear to school each day.

Weather charts have swooping lines on them that look similar to the contour lines on a topographic map. However, these are not lines of equal elevation. They are lines of equal air pressure called isobars.

By looking at the isobars, weather forecasters can tell which way and how fast a front is moving. A front is the leading edge of a pressure system. This helps forecasters predict changes in the weather. But, large weather patterns can affect an entire continent, or even the world. This makes

Today, meteorologists use powerful computers to quickly analyze data and make forecasts.

predicting the weather at your house like trying to find your backyard on a world map!

Like all types of maps, weather charts are only as **accurate** as the information collected for them. And, they are only useful for the purpose for which they are made. So make sure you always have the right type of map for the job!

Weather maps show how pressure systems and other atmospheric conditions work together to create weather patterns.

Understanding Isobars

Parcels of air called pressure systems cause much of our weather. Pressure systems happen when large areas of the earth are heated or cooled. Heated areas produce low-pressure systems. And, cooled areas produce high-pressure systems.

You might hear a forecaster say, "a cold front is approaching." This means cold air is coming your way. If the cold front runs into warm, moist air, the warm air will be forced up out of the way. That is because cold air is denser than warm air. The sudden rise of the lighter, warm air may cause rain and even thunderstorms.

Glossary

accurate - free of errors.

asthma - a condition that causes wheezing and coughing and makes breathing difficult.

cartographer - a maker of maps or charts.

characteristic - a quality or a feature of something.

classify - to arrange in groups or classes, or to sort according to some method or system.

density - the quantity of anything per unit of area.

distribution - the area over which a particular thing is spread.

environment - all the surroundings that affect the growth and well-being of a living thing.

habitat - a place where a living thing is naturally found.

hydrographic survey - a chart with measurements for seas, lakes, rivers, and other bodies of water, especially for navigational use.

passport - a government-issued document that serves to identify a citizen and allows him or her to travel to foreign countries.

plain - a flat or rolling stretch of land without trees.

precinct - a smaller part of a county or a town used in elections.

precipitation - water or the amount of water that falls to the earth as hail, mist, rain, sleet, or snow.

predict - to guess something ahead of time on the basis of observation, experience, or reasoning.

scale - the size of a map, a drawing, or a model compared with what it represents. Also, the equally divided line on a map or a chart that indicates this relationship.

three-dimensional - having the illusion of depth.

unemployment - the state of being without a job. It is also the number of people in a country who do not have jobs.

urban - of or relating to a city.

Web Sites

To learn more about cartography, visit ABDO Publishing Company on the World Wide Web at **www.abdopublishing.com**. Web sites about cartography are featured on our Book Links page. These links are routinely monitored and updated to provide the most current information available.

Index

912   Classifying Maps
Hen   Henzel, Cynthia